DESPERATELY SEEKING SOMEONE

Edited

By

TRUDI RAMM

Illustrated

By

SPENCER HART

First published in Great Britain in 1993 by
ARRIVAL PRESS
1 - 2 Wainman Road, Woodston,
Peterborough, PE2 7BU

All Rights Reserved

Copyright Contributors 1993

Foreword

Desperately Seeking Someone is the perfect book to read before tackling *The Dating Game*. The poems included cover every aspect of the personal adverts that can be found in the classified sections of newspapers: what to write; what to expect from the replies; what has happened to the writers on their dates and more!

Whilst editing this collection I was reminded of all of the trials and tribulations of being single or just looking for companionship. I also found that my colleagues were giving me sidelong glances because 90% of the time I was giggling and even exploded with the odd guffaw! I am sure that you will enjoy reading this light hearted, unusual book as much as I did.

Editor
Trudi Ramm

Contents

Desperately Seeking Someone	Eirlys Roberts	1
Yorkshire	Carol Furlong	2
Chapter and Verse	Lee Newham	2
Past my prime	Roy Sayers	3
Sanitised Hippie	Maggie Camps	3
More Than an Advertisement	Deanna Martin	4
Wonderful Physique	John Noble	4
I Wrote and was Smote	Michael Marshall	6
Lonely Hearts	Christine Isaac	6
Man Required	Sue Hornsby	8
A Simple Request	George Pearson	8
If You're Out There Somewhere	Barbara Henry	10
Is There Anybody Out There	Roy Whitfield	10
Opposites Attract	David Robertson	12
Lovelorn Medallion Man	Marion Helen Corben	12
Ego	Sam Clayton	13
Handsome Knight	Jenny Gibson	13
Elderly Widow	Margaret Elvin-Matthews	14
Wanted	Coleen Hickey	14
Lonely Heart of Croydon	Wendy Roberts	16
Personal Please	Mark Winter	16
A Memo to a Loved One	Anthony B Ogunlowo	17
Sincere man 31	Lynne Gavaghan	17
6532	Vicki Vickers	18
Roulette	Hilary Edwards	18
7pm	Christine Lang	20
Dreaming	David Wood	20
Hopeful	Evelyn Evans	22
Dynamic Executive	D R Watchorn	22
The Lonely Heart	Marjorie Mary Pearson	24
Do Please Help	E Wilcox	24
The Ideal Lady	T Sullivan	25
Personal Ad Quandary	Marion Green	25
Gent - Romantic	D M Hargreaves	26

Dip	Elinor Gordon Lennox	26
Are you There?	Gillian M Thomson	27
Twilight	Sheila McGuire	27
Personal Enquiry	Wendy Winslet	28
Mr Right	Winnie Mayes	28
Where are You	Pauline Crossland	29
Young at Heart	Katherine Delaney	29
The Dating Game	Ted Green	30
RIYP ASAP	J S Rowlands	30
Lonely Heart Box No P7723	Terrence St John	32
What Shall I Say?	Pat Tilley	32
Lonely	Patricia Petres	34
True Love	John Wilson	34
Box 49	Paul Sanders	35
Lonely Heart	Briony V Lill	35
Help	P Lyle	36
Madonna	Les hardy	36
Modest Mr Wonderful	Jan Rusted	37
Big is Beautiful	Glenda White	37
Lasting Love	Cicely heathers	38
Hold my Hand	Heide Hanford	38
Wanted	Fiona Pearl	39
The Ego Trip	S T Fotheringham	39
My Advertisement	Elise M Gibb	40
What a Clown!	Peggy Love	40
I'm Tall, Tanned and Virile	John F Toms	42
I'm Not the Type to Use an Ad	Daniela Ryan	42
I Need a Man...	Catherine P Hall	43
✕ Looking for Love	Jean Stewart	43
Is This you?	Myfyr Foulkes Jones	44
Your Kiss	K Lovejoy	44
Give Me a Call	M M Glancy	45
Personal	Pam Owers	45
Twenty Five Year Old Seeks Soulmate	Leila M Manasseh	46
Love Thy Neighbour	Jean Roberts	46
Ideal Partner!	Harold Hyman	48

Ring me Now	Eric Jeffrey Johnson	48
Personal	Patricia Barr	49
Mature Gentleman	W Owen-Williams	49
Personal	M E Ireland	50
The Middle-Age Prayer	Liz Bramhall	50
Situation Vacant	Lynn Clifford	52
Chinese Birth Signs	Michelle Irving	52
Looking for a Man	Mary Rimmer Pike	54
My Lonely Plea	Vera Hansson	54
Classified	Lisa Starr	56
Love	Eileen Kisby	56
Someone	Mary B Tyrer	57
Madonna Pleasures	Fred Jolly	57
What do I Look for?	Patricia Martindale	58
Destination Destiny	Rhian F Miles	58
Lonely Hearts Ad	Sarah Whitehead	60
Caper Sauce	Marjorie Milton	60
Blind Vision	Anntoinette Dubrett	61
Doubles	Mark Sims	61
What are Friends for?	Meia Allegranza	62
The Night Out	Arthur Monk	62
Starfleet Command	K A Easton	64
Companionship	C R Etheridge	64
I Have Green hair	Hilda Moss	66
Wanted - Someone to Love	Caroline Janney	66
Are you Looking	L Jackson	68
Share With me	Ann Rodgers	68
The Bachelor	Brian Courtman Churcher	69
A Woman Needs a Man	Melanie Burgess	69
It was Arranged	Mitchell	70
Kindred Spirits	J Hickens	70
Requirements of Love	Joan Richardson	71
Seeking	Evelyn Miles	71
Friend of Mine	Cooper	72
Surely	Gillian Ford	72
Chances	S Screen	74
Close Encounters	Tricia Squires	74
Must	J Thomas	76

Looking for Love	George Ponting	76
Little Red Riding Hood	Luke McCann	77
Intermediate Lover Wanted	John Tirebuck	77
Lonely Bachelor Seeks . . .	Patrick Macken	78
Farmer Seeks	Alf Jones	78
Gentle-Man	V A Johnson	79
Footsteps	Ronald Fiske	79
Male Graduate	Peter Higginbotham	80
Lonely Hearts	K J Earnshaw	80
At These Words	Derick Atkins	82
Different Aspects of Love	Bety M Bennett	82
My Kind of Love	Margaret Platt	83
Longing	Kathy Sherratt	83
The Waiting Game	Lewis des Brisay	84
Destiny	Norma Williams	84
Personal Column	Gwyneth Tilley	85
Entice	Mair H Thomas	85
Putting Out Her Stall	Stan Taylor	86
Box No H.O.P.E.	Simone Eade	86
Searching for Love	Lesley Franklin	88
New Man	Sue Challand	88
My Lonely Heart	Ann C Thomas	89
I'm Happy Free and Easy	D T Beeken	89
Wanted	Marian Evans	90
Young at Heart	Maureen Jones	90
Bohemian Rhapsody	Jan Ferrierr	91
Someone	Hazel M Foster	91
The Search	Patricia Short	92
A Soul Companion	J E Gilbert	92
Wanted	Violette Edwards	93
Box 204	William Patrick Hayles	93
Answer to a Dream?	Doris J Baldwin	94
There Must be	P Harris	94
Where is His Wife?	Jacqui Weeks	96

Desperately Seeking Someone

If you need to find a soul-mate, 'cos your sitting on the shelf.
Pick up your local paper, and just simply help yourself.
Amidst the 'Broken Hearted', 'Caring Male' and 'Desperate Dan'.
He must be in there somewhere, the elusive 'Perfect Man'.
'Got no ties? Like to travel?' asks 'wealthy widower, business own'.
Sell the dog! Hide the kids! Put poor mother in a home!
'Retired Gent, Car and Cottage, doesn't smoke and handsome too',
Seeks 'Tall Blonde, Early Twenties', knew he was too good to be
                                                                                  true!
So, I'm filling in the coupon! 'Attractive Lady, tall and trim',
Early Fifties (make that Forty), I'll have to grow a bit, and slim!.

Eirlys Roberts

Yorkshire

Once - desired property - with pleasant, well stocked grounds;
Built in nineteen forty three - looks better than she sounds;
Looking for an owner, prepared to chance his arm;
This 'recently detached' has character and charm.
Inside needs attention - with minimal outlay;
A bargain for the 'hunter' with time to spare each day.
Offers are invited from those who wish to view;
Endless possibilities - should she be sold on you!

Caroline Furlong

Chapter and Verse

I'm a *Hell's Grandad*
With pigtail and Harley,
Who isn't averse to
The odd dozen 'Carlies'.
Want young lady rocker for high-speed
wooing -
And preferably one who's
Ace at tattooing!

Lee Newham

Past my Prime

Sixty years trying to find the right mate
I think I may have left it too late
Just turned seventy nine
And well past my prime
But I still enjoy a blind date

I buy flowers to entice them to bed
But all they want is to get wed
And at my time of life
The last thing I need is a wife
Just a woman who's easily led

Roy Sayers

Sanitised Hippie

Sanitised hippie of forty six
still smokes cigs but no booze or trips!
Seeks similar guy whose learnt something from past
like me, bad news, but wants next chapter to last
with help of good books, conversation, art -
helping addicts maybe - we can play our part
So if you're seeking an interesting new life -
I'm not too lost in good causes to be a good wife!

Maggie Camps

More Than an Advertisement

What do you get from a Personal Ad?
Cheering up when you're sad,
A vision of hope,
To a change in your life,
Or a friend you can count on,
In trouble and strife,
Someone to share,
In your secrets and sorrows,
Someone to laugh with,
And share your tomorrows.

Deanna Martin

Wonderful Physique

I've got a wonderful physique,
My muscles are as hard as teak,
I've also got a high IQ,
And manners that would impress you.

I've got a villa in the sun,
A very keen sense of good fun,
I might exaggerate its true,
But then I think that you might too!

John Noble

I Wrote and was Smote

I decided to write
In reply to your plea,
A lonely invite
That appealed to me.
Attractive widow
Living alone,
Feeling low
In an empty home.
'Love at first sight,' people said.
And within a week we were wed.

Michael Marshall

Lonely Hearts

I place my advert so full of hope
And send it to the lonely hearts column
Then I wait for the replies to come
I hope to meet my perfect match
But second best is better than none
A reply arrives and we arrange to meet
And there was instant attraction between us
We are the perfect match and we fall in love
On the day we wed you made me the happiest bride
And we promised to love until the day we died.

Christine Isaac

Man Required

Man required: To love and care
For two children and a
Woman fair.
If you like chaos
Laughter too
Then write to me
C/o Box 202.

Sue Hornsby

A Simple Request

A gentle love I now desire.
Of your response, so I enquire.

These are the messages I seek:
love's invitation on your cheek;
love's fragrance captured in a dress;
love's sympathy when hands caress;
love's solace from your finger tips;
love's burden taken on your lips;
love's pleasure in soft eyes at play;
love's passion in a month's delay.

George Pearson

If You're Out There Somewhere

If you're male, height five feet eight and aged around fifty three,
Then once you've read my advert, perhaps you'll write to me.
Ideally you should live close by, say within a couple of miles.
Though one thing that's a real must is, you should have a friendly
                                                                        smile.
A love of pop and jazz music would also be a winner,
As would going for a social drink, followed by a quiet dinner.
Country walks would be a pleasure, as would spending time at home,
But if distance made it hard to meet, we could keep in touch by
                                                                        phone.
So if you've read this simple verse and feel vaguely interested in me.
I'll close by simply adding that my age is forty-seven,
While my height is five feet three.

Barbara Henry

Is There Anybody Out There

Wanted, someone to love
To be my wife
To share my life
Must be caring
Honest and sharing
Someone to scheme
And dream
Towards happiness
Together
If you're out there
I'm here
Waiting

Roy Whitfield

Opposites Attract

I'm looking for a husband
'Cause my other one he lacked
He was too similar to me
And it's opposites that attract.

He's got to have lots of money
'Cause I'm not very rich
And he must be the perfect gentleman
'Cause I'm a right old bitch.

David Robertson

Lovelorn Medallion Man

I saw you seated at the bar in your high-heeled cowboy boots;
I saw your blonde-streaked shaggy hair and noticed its dark roots.
I saw the rings upon your hands and their cheap gaudiness -
Matching the shocking style of your outmoded dress.
I saw your shirt unbuttoned to expose your hairy chest
Where, swinging from a bright gold chain, a medallion came to rest.
I saw the flower that you wore for easy recognition
But when I saw your flashy smile, I knew with firm decision
The 'lovelorn' Ad I'd answered with anticipated glee
Might have been news yesterday but, now, it's history!

Marion Helen Corben

Ego

Once I was blind, but now I see
That loneliness is not for me.
I long for someone, thoughtful, kind;
Careful, with a trusting mind;
Slowly to anger, quick to praise,
Tolerant in many ways.
To such a one, could she be found,
Constant in the daily round,
Charming, plain, petite or tall,
I'd give my love, my life, my all.

Sam Clayton

Handsome Knight

He was dressed in khaki when I met him
A soldier on leave during war
He was tall he was blond he was handsome
All that I'd dreamed of and more

I knew then that I need look no further
Than this handsome knight here at my side
The following summer we married
There was never a more loving bride.

Jenny Gibson

Vis sister

Elderly Widow

Elderly Widow? I'm telling the truth,
Gone from my mirror all traces of youth,
But I'm hoping that someone reads between the lines,
I'm not looking for romance, or jolly good times,
I want a companion, someone to share
The long empty evenings now nobody's there,
To reminisce of our youth, and the things we have done,
The children we've raised, our departed loved ones,
To comfort each other, and not be afraid,
Of the reaper of time, who's waiting off stage.

Margaret Elvin-Matthews

Wanted

Tall, good-looking, professional male
with his own car and house (and something to sail)
Very intelligent with excellent dress-sense
and good conversation, always in the correct tense.
Sexy and clean with sweet-smelling aftershave
Generous and kind, who knows how to behave.
A gentleman: standing and opening doors -
A masculine man, but who'll help with the chores.
Somewhere out there you've got to be waiting
for a girl just like me with whom to start dating.

Coleen Hickey

Lonely Heart of Croydon

Lonely heart of Croydon seeking someone for romance
A wealthy, sexy, businessman who dares to take a chance
Now anyone with half of this is surely going to be
Engaged, in jail, a dad to many, anything but free
Despite the effort of this search and high rate of divorce
We humans yearn to find a mate to call our own of course
I'd like to know just what response these adverts do create
Who makes inquiries then proceeds beyond the second date
So are these ads successful can one really find perfection
By writing one's requirements in the 'Sun's Classified Section?'

Wendy Roberts

Personal Please

Lonely, bored, despairing
Looking for someone who's caring
Hope you're good looking
Enjoy home cooking
Like to go out
Have fun no doubt
Seeking a friend
Maybe marriage at end
Photo with your reply
A good night, on me you can rely

Mark Winter

A Memo to a Loved One

I hope you are true,
I hope you are real,
I want to hold you forever in my arms,
And never let you go and to me
it'll be like feeling
the sun on both sides,
and my tan would be the best in town.

Who could ask for more?

Anthony B Ogunlowo

Sincere Man 31

'Sincere Man 31
Wishes to meet lady 24 - 30
View friendship/marriage.'
A little voice said 'Write to him'.
The lonely girl penned a letter to her future
A letter, a phone call, a date;
Friendship blossomed, love grew,
Smiles came again.
September '86 in Autumn's glory,
Wedding bells rang - a true story!

Lynne Gavaghan

6532

Where did you get to Jimmy?
Did you remember the sixth?
Was Jenny on time when she met you,
On the steps near the church of St Nick's?

I hope you were gallant and mannered,
And treated her gently with care.
When the bill for the meal was debated,
I hope you didn't say, 'Share'.

If the answer to this lot was 'Yes',
Please ring - 6532 . . . Your Next Guest.

Vicki Vickers

Roulette

The glittering prizes await
In Saturday Rendezvous.
Witty, charming and intelligent,
In these columns, they say.
Tall attractive lawyer,
Looking for someone mature;
Could it be me?
I'll take ten years off my age;
I'm not slim and thirty-five.
But love's a game: winner takes all, you see.

Hilary Edwards

7pm

7pm
Walking to meet you
Wondering what
You'll look like
Wondering why
You want to meet me
Wondering whether
You'll be there.

Christine Lang

Dreaming

Dreaming of perfection . . . for me the only one
Never mind rejection for that is half the fun
So many faces, so many places
Until the deed is done . . .
Will I find her here? Will I find her there?
Page forty three in the box - I'd like to care and share
She's had three hundred letters (I sent them all - beware!)
I'm reaching for perfection to be my lifelong wife
I'm addicted - need injection! - To fix my single life . . .

David Wood

Hopeful

'Hello', my name is Chris.
I am looking for a Miss
Attractive and smart
Who could lose her heart
I would like a 'homely' girl
Romantic - a real live pearl
Not over twenty-eight.
Won't you ring and make a date?

Evelyn Evans

Dynamic Executive

Tall, professional, solvent male
Quite something in the city,
Finds himself alone at night,
Oh isn't it a pity!
So if you're a slim, attractive blonde,
With the appropriate qualifications
Write to me now, without delay
And I'll meet your aspirations.

D R Watchorn

The Lonely Heart

Wanted. Someone to love me
I've been on my own for so long
the urge to have some affection
has been surging up very strong.
Being a widow is lonely
with just my cat as companion
I'd like to go out with a man
to show my friends he's a champion.
Those who apply please note
I might fall in love and marry them.

Marjorie Mary Pearson

Do Please Help

Do please help me if you can
All I need is a macho man
There's something lacking in my life
Doesn't someone need a wife?
I'd like him healthy and wealthy
Good looking with all his own teeth.
I know that I'm asking quite a deal
But he also must have sex appeal.
On reflection - perhaps it's an impossible dream
Could there be a man like that to be seen?

E Wilcox

The Ideal Lady

The ideal lady
Just for me
Should be passionate and
Good company

Age is not too important
As long as she looks good
I'm in my twenties and
Blessed with hot blood.

T Sullivan

Personal Ad Quandary

I read them and wonder 'why?'
Yet, perhaps, should I try?
Reply?
Or advertise
To realise
A friend, the kind
Alike in thought and mind.

Or find
Hope to provoke
An infinite joke!

Marion Green

Gent - Romantic

Gent - romantic - seventy plus
Seeks lady - kind and generous
To put a little spice and kick
Into 'adventurous' walking stick.
According to the cardiograph
Time awaits yet many a laugh.
Would dearly love to find a mate
Before St Peter clangs the gate.
Somewhere out there must be my 'Joan'
Searching for her cornerstone.

D M Hargreaves

Dip

I wonder if there is no one,
Or anyone, or who would know
Of someone who could be delighted
To meet me? I feel there, out there
A person is waiting to be found
Quite without taking - are you around?
Someone who loves, with no forgetting.
Afterwards who'll fill a life of loneliness,
Perhaps a meal ad infinitum,
Or fill me into relaxation?

Elinor Gordon Lennox

Are you There?

You're out there somewhere, this I know,
And if you're lonely just like me,
Drop me a line and tell me so,
Then firm friends we can be.

I'm looking for someone to share,
A three-week ocean cruise.
So do you think you'd fit the bill?
Come on, you've nothing to lose.

Gillian M Thomson

Twilight

She wanted a companion, a man to hold her hand,
A shoulder she could lean on, someone to understand.
She didn't want a husband, just someone who would share
Her love of life in general, a man for whom she'd care.
She offered true affection, and maybe real romance;
Her sense of humour bubbled, she longed to sing and dance!
Perhaps they'd dine and travel, or take a country walk,
She hoped they'd go to concerts, then quietly sit and talk.
She placed the ad and found her man, he suited perfectly,
For he was only eighty four, whilst she was eighty three!

Sheila McGuire

Personal Enquiry

I am female and forty, nearly forty one,
I am looking around to have some fun
I am short with dark hair, plump and wear glasses
Anyone similar automatically passes
Someone whose laugh is not really forced
Someone who's single or maybe divorced
Conversation to be somewhat respectable
Humour and intelligence quite acceptable
A photo we will post before a fixed date
Then just turn up clean and tidy but never be late.

Wendy Winslet

Mr Right

Man mid forties, was what first caught my eye.
When I actually met him, his fiftieth birthday was nigh.
Tall dark and handsome, was what the advert said,
Short fat and hairy, was what he was instead.
A nice home, car and money were mentioned in the ad.
Grotty flat, rusty wreck and UB were really what he had.
I think I'll stick to dreaming of finding 'Mr Right'
Instead of answering 'Lonely Hearts', I won't get such a fright.

Winnie Mayes

Where are you

Must be at least six foot tall,
Good looks do not bother me at all,
Plenty of money is a must,
A life style, I will adjust,
The age gap large enough to say,
There is at least one foot in the grave,
I will love and cherish you to the end,
Then for my toy boy I will send.

Pauline Crossland

Young at Heart

Elegant, widowed lady who's just turned sixty-three
Seeks a well-preserved unattached gentleman for company
To form a lasting friendship to span our twilight years
Someone special to share with me the laughter and the tears
Like me, you will be caring, young at heart and full of fun
So if you'd like to hear from me contact Box 101.

Katherine Delaney

The Dating Game

The dating game, where do you start?
You're past, the *sell by* date,
But read on, take heart.

If you fit the criteria, you can answer the ad,
A ready made family, you could be the new dad?
A religious preference, or point of view,
Is an attraction to some, could that be you?
Age is a factor, important to some,
Non smoker required, if, you answer this one.
A bimbo, a toyboy, a really good friend,
We are, all seeking, the same, in the end.

Ted Green

RIYP ASAP

I'm single and I'm lonely, I've a multitude of cats
I'm very fond of gardening but scared to death of rats.
I'm shy and slightly rounded perhaps a little plump.
But no so unattractive that I could be called a frump.
I don't want you if you're bossy or an argumentative fumer
I just want someone cuddly with a lovely sense of humour.

J S Rowlands

Lonely Heart Box No P7723

(With apologies to Maud)

Dear lonely heart, I'm waiting,
Waiting like him, at the gate,
I've tickets for two at the flowershow,
Plus a candlelight dinner at eight -
In the personal ads I found you,
Your voice over the phone
Was a thrill,
So I'll be waiting,
Waiting, waiting,
With a big bunch of daffodils.

Terrence St John

What Shall I Say?

What shall I say? Hair going grey
Or shall I put mature and caring
Shall I put intelligent or is that irrelevant
Or shall I say, young at heart, daring.

Who am I looking for, car owner, non smoker?
Tall, short or does it much matter
Do I want romance or simply a friendship
And do I let on that I chatter.

I have it: mature, fun loving gal
Seeks gentleman similar for possible pal.

Pat Tilley

Lonely

Alone in my room feeling sad and solemn
Composing an advert for the Personal Column.
No one could ever take your place
But life is empty without you and hard to face.

'Lonely widow, 60's, stylish and slim.
Loves music, the theatre, to dine and to swim,
Enjoys walks in the countryside and Old Tyme Dance,
Is searching for happiness and lasting romance.'

Soulmate wanted to share laughter and love,
Oh please answer my prayer, dear Lord above!

Patricia Petres

True Love

True love is what I look for,
true love for you and me
true love that's everlasting
forever it will be.
You're always there beside me
you even hold my hand
you always gently guide me
through the barren land
true love is what I look for
true love is you and me.

John Wilson

Box 49

A rich man would like to meet the woman of his dreams,
A countryman who never works has land and many schemes.
I often fly abroad for business trips and many things,
A trip to hotter climes than here is just one of my whims.
Alas I have no money in the bank - I'm on the dole,
I have no land at all to farm - no country squire role.
But if you're thirty something and like a simple time,
I'd like to write to you as views and life sound just like mine.
So please now stop your searching and write to me a line,
Just a photo and your details marked box number 49.

Paul Sanders

Lonely Heart

I am a lady who would like
    To meet a gentleman,
So please dear advert do your best
    And help me if you can.
He doesn't need to have good looks -
    Be hunky, bronzed or tall;
But feeling lonely just like me,
    And if he is - to call.

My box number is 27;
To know my age just add 11.

Briony V Lill

Help

Love must not pass me by
So again I will try and try
Is there a man out there?
With whom I might share
The ups and downs of life
I want to be a wife!
I will laugh and cry with you
I won't be blue if you are true
I am neither fat nor thin, rich nor poor
But this I know I must have love once more.

P Lyle

Madonna

A Cleopatra I don't need, just a fun-loving woman of gentle breed.
Music and dancing with a flair for words,
So we can gel, like two love birds.
Minds on the same track,
If needs be, fight the world, back to back.

Simple taste with a homely flair,
We can build a Heaven to share,
I don't think I'm asking for much,
For a woman with the Madonna touch.
So if you think you 'fit' the bill answer this ad', 'I'll be yours at will.'

Les Hardy

Modest Mr Wonderful

I'm handsome and self assured it seems,
An answer to any Ladies dreams,
I play golf and I sail boats
I need a Lady who on me dotes,
No strings, no ties, no ball and chain,
A lady whose needs are just the same,
Independent, but not too clever,
No guarantee, it will last forever.

Jan Rusted

Big is Beautiful

I'm a cuddly lady and I'm sick of men who sneer,
'Oh, you're overweight are you?' and then they disappear.
So the man I seek won't object to this,
Gable looks would be a help, but 'Hey, don't kiss like a wet fish!'
A moustache is a must, if it suits the face,
He can buy me lingerie, especially trimmed with lace.
He should like music, talk, and meals in bed,
If he starts complaining, 'Watch it man you're dead',
He must be truly devoted, or I won't waste my time
Anyone out there reading this, do drop me a line.

Glenda White

Lasting Love

I'm looking for excitement.
Lots of fun and romance.
Someone to cuddle by moonlight,
Our heads in the clouds while we dance.
Hear the wedding bells ringing,
Just to let all the world know,
We could be so very happy.
With our two hearts aglow.
Will our love last forever?
Yes if we truly trust each other.
That's what I ask from my lover.

Cicely Heathers

Hold my Hand

Life's fun - good job - great friends,
But home and heart are bare.
I miss the tender hands
Of someone who will care,
Who'll laugh and cry with me and hold me tight,
Whom I can love and cherish day and night.
He should have joie de vivre, an agile mind,
Love music, nature, travel and be kind,
Enjoy city's highlife and the peace of the land;
Happy anywhere as long as you hold my hand.

Heide Hanford

Wanted

Wanted: unconditional love,
A friend to share my joys and fears,
Someone who will disregard
The failure of my wasted years.

A mate who will not criticise
Attempts to mend a broken life,
A concrete block for crumbling wall,
Wanted: unconditional wife.

Fiona Pearl

The Ego Trip

Single man aged twenty-four
Seeks friendship first, then maybe more
From single woman, who enjoys
The company of men, not boys.
A stunner he can take on dates:
Paraded to impress his mates.
An ego trip that's good in bed,
That mirrors pictures in his head
Of what the perfect bird has got:
With such a partner? Not a lot . . .

S T Fotheringham

My Advertisement

I am an unattached woman of five and fifty years
I've had my ups and downs in life and had my wear and tear
I'm five foot six in my stockinged feet my hair is brown my dress is
neat
I speak quite well although on my own, as you could tell if me you'd
phone.
I have a sense of humour too - though sometimes hidden well
And there's no truth in the rumour, as far as I can tell
That *I* am more than past *it* - in fact I'm in my prime
And *if* and *when* the right man comes along
He'll find out, all in, good time.

Elise M Gibb

What a Clown!

'I bike,' it said
'I hike,' it said
'I dance and fly my own plane.'

He's no slob, I thought
Just the job, I thought
Seems he also has a brain!

What a clown, I was
How let down, I was
Left standing alone in the rain.

Peggy Love

I'm Tall, Tanned and Virile

I'm tall, tanned, virile and healthy,
But certainly not, materially wealthy,
True love, kindness and laughter,
I would give in good measure,
To a loving attractive girl,
Who, I would treasure forever.

John F Toms

I'm Not the Type to Use an Ad

But if it ever came to that,
I'd go for a precious age-old thing -
true love, it beats everything!
   Flowers, sweet nothings, romantic treats,
   cuddles galore; I swear it beats
   everything else in this world -
   which love makes go round -
   if truth be told.

Daniela Ryan

I Need a Man . . .

I need a man,
to hold my hand.
I need a man,
to understand.

I need a man,
for cuddles and passion.
I need a man,
who gives compassion.

I need a man,
to talk to.
I need a man,
is it you?

Catherine P Hall

Looking for Love

Man seeks friendship, man seeks wife,
Seeks new home, new start in life
With lady who likes theatres, pubs,
Likes outings, dancing, likes nightclubs.
Together we could cut a rug,
Together we'd be nice and snug.
Together we could take a chance,
Take my number for romance.

Jean Stewart

Is This you?

A jolly disposition, lots of love to give,
Thoughtful, kind and willing,
Love to really live.
Honest and truthful, full of care,
Full of affection, like to share,
A smile that reflects the beauty in life.
Then you are the replica,
Of my dear wife.

Myfyr Foulkes Jones

Your Kiss

To you this note my one last hope
My love, my soul, my cure
A chance to live a life bespoke
So bright, so light, so pure
Write back to me and we shall meet
Sweet promise to elope
No more my wounded heart to treat
Restore and make my life complete
Your kiss my antidote

K Lovejoy

Give Me a Call

I don't want to be alone for the rest of my life
All I really want is to be somebody's wife,
I may not be tall, I may not be thin,
But I'm still capable of loving a man,
I may not be beautiful, nor stand out in a crowd,
But what's in a body, if there's nothing inside,
I'm honest, I'm loyal, I'm romantic as well,
I know you're out there somewhere,
So why not give me a call.

M M Glancy

Personal

Female, blue eyed, a blonde but dyed,
Requires a mate for steady date
Who likes to dance and disco prance
'Don't want a meet with two left feet',
A car I'd like or motorbike
But I won't fuss if train and bus,
Wants to huddle in a cuddle
'If tall in socks I'll bring a box'
I like to smile, am versatile
Please read my plea and contact me.

Pam Owers

Twenty Five Year Old Seeks Soulmate

Wanted - a husband for a home-loving girl
He need not be wealthy, a Prince or an Earl
Just a hardworking guy who will give it a whirl
With a pretty young lady whose first name is Pearl

Her hobbies are many; she loves music best
She swims and plays tennis, solves crosswords with zest.

She is caring, vivacious and fun-loving too
If she finds 'Mr Right' she will always be true
To that special young man - is it possibly you?
To find out, get in touch without further ado!

Leila M Manasseh

Love Thy Neighbour

She'd loved him with a vengeance
born of passion, from the start,
The boy next door had moved away
and vanished, with her heart.
They said he'd gone to Devon.

Reduced to scanning 'Lonely Hearts',
whilst struggling with her sadness,
An ad she spied, read, 'Suzy,
Give me half a chance? It's madness.'
The coward from number seven!

Jean Roberts

CLUE (15 ACROSS): "WE WANNA BE ......"

Ideal Partner!

I replied to the want ads excitedly
In the search for a partner acceptable to me
I'd found someone I felt 'fitted the bill'
A fun loving person who sounded quite 'brill!'
Someone who had money and status and looks
Whose interests encompassed world travel and books.
The one I was sure would suit me just fine
That is till I realised . . . the advert was mine!
The moral we learn from this sad sorry rhyme . . .
Economy of truth lets you down every time!

Harold Hyman

Ring me Now

The hair so fair and full of lustre
Her eyes so bright and yes so loving
The smile shines forth, the radiance glowing
All sadness gone and hope is showing
In love her charm is so rewarding
Her faith renewed! A new day dawning
If this is you? It well may be.
Please ring me now - just let us see.
What love can do for you and me
That we may share in eternity.

Eric Jeffrey Johnson

Personal

I advertised in the local News
for a companion warm and friendly
someone loyal to care for me
no need for him to be trendy
the Postman brought a big response
when I read the mail I decided at once
his photograph said it all
I picked up the phone and made the call
now he shares his life with me
this black and white mongrel
by the name of scruffy.

Patricia Barr

Mature Gentleman

Mature gentleman wishes to meet
Sophisticated lady (remember the air?)
With view to placing at her feet
Fondest affection and faithful care . . .
Hope springs eternal, or so they say,
To ease the hurt that lingers on.
Would like to walk out on yesterday
With someone caring, would lavish upon
All a frustrated soul's devotion
So far adrift on a lonely sea . . .

W Owen-Williams

Personal

You don't have to be a rich man,
you don't have to be a saint.
You can down the old odd pinta, but
don't pretend to be what you 'aint'.
Just show that you've got a heart dear,
that's honest, and warm, and true.
Then we'll leave the rest to fate, and
just hope that I'm right for you.

M E Ireland

The Middle-Age Prayer

Dear God, who made the stars above
Please, send to me a man to love.
Short and fat . . . thin or tall,
Really, it doesn't matter at all.
And he shan't mind that my parts, once fit,
Through wear and tear have sagged and slipped.
But both will see the hearts within
That life and time, nor age will dim
Preferably before I pass for thirty
With the glow of candle light behind me!

Liz Bramhall

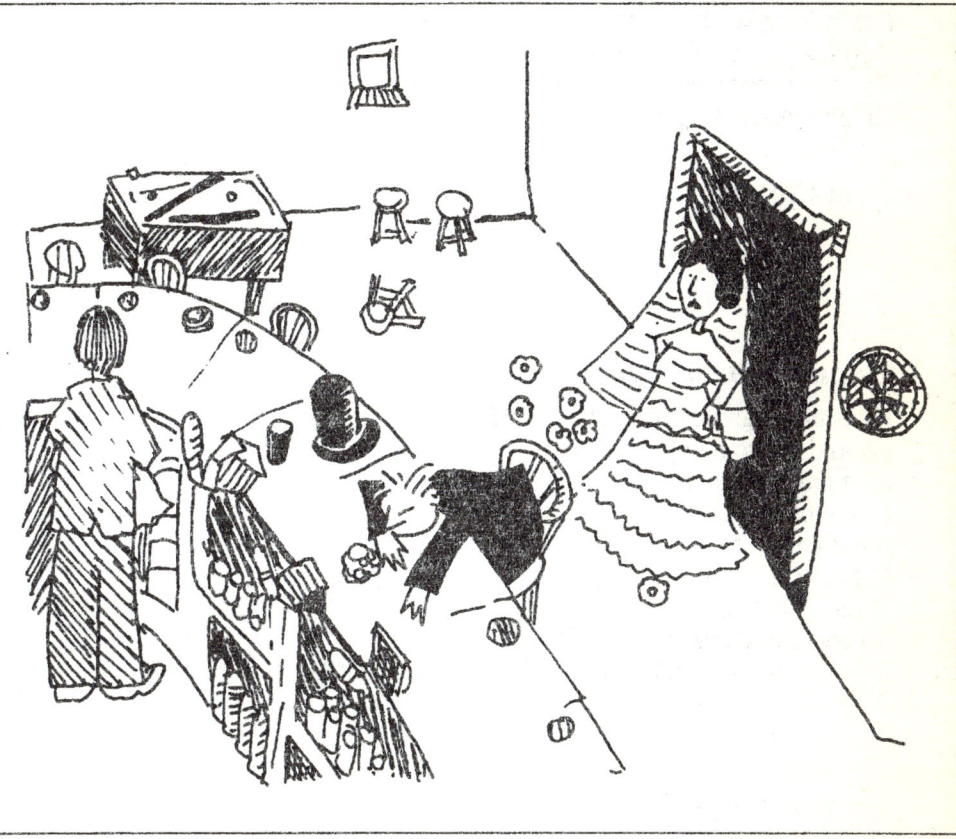

Situation Vacant

'A vacancy exists . . . ' read the advert,
'For a toy-boy, aged twenty-one plus.
No experience necessary,
Just a body driven by lust!
Full training will be given.
If you're interested, please apply
To box number three seven seven.
Or 'phone and I'll give you a try.'

Lynn Clifford

Chinese Birth Signs

Nice man wanted born 1952 or 1953
I would like to meet a snake
Or a dragon like me
I have been out with a dog
A pig and a rat
But they're not very happy men
Their humour's quite flat
So come and make me smile
And I'm sure you will agree
That you have never met a dragon
As nice as me.

Michelle Irving

Looking for a Man

I'm in the personal ads this week.
I'm looking for a *man*.
A red-hot male would suit me fine,
So find one if you can.
He needn't be a Rambo,
Or even play the flute.
There's just one main requisite
That he has a lot of . . . *loot*.

Mary Rimmer Pike

My Lonely Plea

I'm looking for a 'fella' whose got a turn of wit,
He must be quite good looking
He also must be fit.
I'm a good looking girl with a very neat waist,
I like theatres and parties and have very good taste.
My age is four and twenty,
As for money - I've got plenty.
So please apply as soon as poss,
But do remember - I'll be *boss*.

Vera Hansson

Classified

Caring, single mother, of twenty years old,
Fun loving, attractive, so I've been told.
Seeks friendship, fun, and possible romance,
With any male willing to give me a chance.
Between twenty-five and thirty, a photo's a must,
Tall, dark and handsome, someone to trust,
So if you like children, you know what to do,
For happiness contact, PO Box 22.

Lisa Starr

Love

I need a partner
Who is strong and true
Whose love will never die
Who will take me
For his bride
To be a friend with lots of fun
Who enjoys the things
The same as me
That is love

Eileen Kisby

Someone

I am in my prime an unattached female
Interested in dancing, poetry, art
Would like to meet tall attractive male
Who'd get on with me, right from the start
The special chap, must have a great sense of fun
Wine me, dine me when day's work is done
Go for long walks with my 'Jack Russell' at heel
Put up with son's demand for a meal!
An eighteen year old cat, called 'Rosie' poor thing
That certain man, could make my heart sing.

Mary B Tyrer

Madonna Pleasures

Single female seeks the hand of a friend
To help her forget a romance at an end
It must be a male no older than thirty
Considerate and kind without being flirty
I am a blonde with a very full figure
Just like Madonna, only very much bigger
He must be single with only friendship to start
And have the ability to mend my broken heart
If he succeeds in this initial endeavour
He may go on to win all my full figure pleasure.

Fred Jolly

What do I Look for?

What do I look for in love?
A person with understanding
Who will guide me in all I do,
Walk with me and talk with me
Thrill me through and through.

Stay with me through ups and downs
Accept me as I am, even the frowns,
Growing older together
Finding stronger feelings,
Faithful friend and lover.

Patricia Martindale

Destination Destiny

Sally read the paper, scoured the personal ad', and questioned
                                        what to do,
Her marriage failed, no partner now, past lovers far and few.
The dial code, a local address - 'what harm to ring the lad?'
She questioned in her deepest thoughts, 'am I really going mad?'
Sally plucked up courage, and dialled the number in the paper,
A cheery reply, more than she'd hoped, sought forth from casual
                                                caper.
The two met up on sunny day, and toured local surround,
And to their delight, in tinted sight, found love once lost now found.
So now betrothed, always loved never loathed, they court in
                                                harmony,
And wonder was that local ad' for 'Purrfect Partners' really their
                                                destiny.

Rhian F Miles

Lonely Hearts Ad

Are you feeling lonely
With nowhere to go
Others enjoying life
Which surely you well know
Come to the lonely hearts club
Enjoy our times of fun
And hopefully very soon
Your happiness will have begun

Sarah Whitehead

Caper Sauce

As the lonely, loveless years did slowly pass me by -
It seemed to me that I did nought but sigh
Until that day, when in the paper, an ad led me on a merry caper -
This man, it seemed, was a lonely man -
Cultured, young and handsome - a living Peter Pan
With trembling fingers and racing heart - it mattered not we
                                                            were miles apart
The 'phone was sticky in my hands - I knew not what to say
The only thing I knew for sure was an urgent need to pray -
That voice I heard - it made me sad - nay, more than that it made
                                                                                me mad
For 'twas none other than that of my dear old Dad.

Marjorie Milton

Blind Vision

Tall, blue-eyed blonde, Scandinavian and lover of the Arts,
Was how he had described himself in column 'Lonely Hearts'.
My dream man, my Adonis, my soul mate,
The Gods really had stepped in, and truly sealed my fate.

The man I met in Peacock Hue, is still inside my heart,
But all that's left 'to have and to hold'
Are a few missing and perished parts.

His locks of gold have faded away, yet in love's memory I hold,
His cherished love, when he smiles at me,
I would not change him for a thousand crocks of Gold.

Anntoinette Dubrett

Doubles

I am a male,
not yet stale,
who likes his ale.

Are you a lass
with some class,
who likes a glass.

Got a bob or two
will share with you,
if you'll be true.

Mark Sims

What are Friends for?

I didn't want to do it, my best friend forced me,
'No one will be serious about it' I told her over a cup of tea,

Annoyed at my friend's determined persistence,
I let down the wall and my weakening resistance.

Can the newspaper really contain love and not war?
Before I rang up I thought, '. . . What am I doing this for?'

So many ads, which one should I choose,
I am so lonely now, I've got nothing to lose.

Blindfolded my pen landed on his advert, third time lucky so they say,
Who would of thought it would lead to our wedding day . . .?

Meia Allegranza

The Night Out

Would someone, please reply, to this lament,
Colour, size or age irrelevant,
Ten Pin bowling seems a dream,
Or failing that, the bowling green.

A walk around the local park,
Watching the wild fowl, 'til it's dark,
Your company is what I need,
Please someone, somewhere, hear me plead.

My age, before you knock the door,
Is three months short of ninety four!

Arthur Monk

Starfleet Command

Star Fleet Command from UK Starship Female Dual Role;
Regret inform departure of male co-control.
Although maintaining orbit, with fellow crewman gone
Uncertain how much longer this state can carry on.
Approaching forty, please excuse archaic 'in full flower';
All phaser banks still throbbing, with full computer power;
Yet urgent need for rescue by one who'll sympathise
Whilst guiding helm; with strong physique, compassionate and wise.
He'll find all cabins shipshape, and coping with the work -
Just SOS and Mayday in despatching Captain Kirk!

K A Easton

Companionship

In our twilight years we met
Through the classified
We were satisfied
Danced at the Palais
Went to the ballet
And the Halle
Candlelit dinner for two
She went down with the flu
Nurse shook her head
I took to my bed

C R Etheridge

I Have Green Hair

I have green hair, (I'm twenty stone)
A deaf aid and big glasses
My hobbies, Bunjee jumping
And ballet dancing classes
A male for friend or travel scene
Though I long to be a bride
In case you miss me when we meet
A photograph supplied
My appearance . . . all invention
Wrote like this to draw attention.

Hilda Moss

Wanted - Someone to Love

'Someone to love me'.
Someone to care,
Someone to hug me,
Someone to be there.
Stood with my arms around his shoulder,
Keeping me warm, and me, getting bolder,
Making it clear and to appear,
I want him today and every day,
of the year.

Caroline Janney

Are you Looking

Are you looking for a life-long friend
Or a stranger on your path
Someone to cherish dearly
Or a pal to have a laugh
Are you searching for a partner
To share your grief and woes
Or just someone to dance with
That sings the songs you know.

L Jackson

Share With me

Come stay with me
And share my nest,
Share my living
And share my rest.
Help with the cooking
And the washing up.
Drink the wine
From my loving cup.
Come share with me
My partner be.

Ann Rodgers

The Bachelor

I'm lonely now, at forty five, and living on my own,
With no-one here to share my life and help me plan my days.
So I've decided now's the time to venture into print,
And post an ad - you'll think I'm mad! -
Which says I need a pretty maid to help me mend my ways.

The girl I have in mind, you see, is tall and lissom, blonde,
With all the cultured ways that go to make a cultured life.
The trouble I foresee arises when I take her home
To a council flat, so humble that
She never could consent to be a humble dustman's wife!

Brian Courtman Churcher

A Woman Needs a Man

What do I want in a man?
At my age you cannot be fussy.
Forget the film-looks if I can
And settle for personality.

Romantic goes without saying
But it is costly in this day and age.
What has love got to do with it anyway,
We pick out our men from the printed page.

Melanie Burgess

It was Arranged

It was arranged, I wore a rose.
To impress I carried prose.
I sat and ordered coffee white.
Then found the light was much too bright.
I sought the shade to compliment.
Then sprayed again my dearest scent.
I was prepared but where were you?
Then ordered coffee number two.
Abandoned by the errant rose.
I sat and read my book of prose.

Mitchell

Kindred Spirits

'Young at heart lady' wants to relate.
To a similar person.
Perhaps a soul mate.

Someone who loves nature
Trees, flowers and things
Gardens, plants, birds and I love to sing.

I've given up smoking
I can't drive a car
But please reply soon -
Whoever you are.

J Hickens

Requirements of Love

At fourteen years he had to be
Dashing, good looking, creating awe -
At twenty-two, the same poor chap
Made me wonder what I saw.
At thirty-six my ideal man, helps
Out with children all he can!
At fifty he must still have lots of go,
And treat me - not often saying *no*!
At sixty-three, I've got it right.
He's true, he's loyal, and a lovely sight.

Joan Richardson

Seeking

Mutual bonding
      of spirit
Yet free
      to be
Just you
      and me
These things
      I seek
Sharing, caring
      in love.

Evelyn Miles

Friend of Mine

It's lovely to know you are always there
Whenever I'm in trouble or despair
True friends are very hard to find
That's why I appreciate you, friend of mine.

We've known each other for many years
You make me laugh when I'm near to tears.
We've had our ups and had our downs
We've acted like a couple of clowns
But nothing has ever torn us apart
Because we are friends to the very heart.

Let it be this way 'til the end of time
Because I've got used to you, friend of mine.

Cooper

Surely

Surely there must be a man out there
With eyes brown or green, hair dark or fair,
A man who adores art, music and books
(Much more important than wealth or good looks.)
An egalitarian who is thoughtful and kind and
Giving in affection (without, always 'other things' in mind).
With deep sensitivity, a sense of good fun,
With an uninflated ego - are you the one?
If all the above strikes a chord in your heart
Contact me now, let the relationship start.

Gillian Ford

Chances

I'm looking for someone warm and sincere,
Someone to love me and call me his dear
Are you the one I could give my heart to?
Please don't be shy get in touch, do.

I love Mozart, Beethoven and Elvis too
This music I hope I could share with you.
I'll tell you my secrets if you tell me yours
Between us both we may open new doors.

S Screen

Close Encounters

I'd built up my hopes - expectations ran high
But when he stepped from his car, I just wanted to die!
He waddled towards me, yellow teeth a-glowing
A fat belly from beneath a tight T-shirt showing.

I rehearsed my excuses - 'My Aunt has just died . . . '
When a cream coated voice spoke up at my side.
'Hi! I'm Peter from Peterborough - you must be my date.'
I gazed up at Adonis - I just knew this was fate.

I must phone my Aunt and tell her I might be home late . . .

Tricia Squires

Must

Needed one Prince Charming
Tall, dark handsome etc
Must be able to ignore
The dogs dirt on the path (next door's)
The messy home (half-term you know)
The pile of dirty washing (it's raining again)
The child running wild (no real reason)
My general insanity (caused by above mentioned)
If my charming prince should stay (more than two hours)
Then life time romance, matrimony a must.

J Thomas

Looking for Love

When young Folk 'wed', they have in mind,
to make their World, as often said,
'A Heaven on Earth', where Peace they'll find,
and make their lives as they would wish,
Love each other, and on Each bestow,
A Love so great, like a Heavenly Glow.

George Ponting

Little Red Riding Hood

Little Red Riding Hood
freed by Wolf Man
looking for Prince Charming
who's over twenty one
who likes sports
All on my lonesome
Seeks Hero
To share Weekday and Evenings
Breakfast, dinner and tea.

Luke McCann

Intermediate Lover Wanted

Wanted. Replacement bookend to complete a matching pair.
Months of desperation on the clock. Upholstery showing wear.
Shouldn't really be doing this. Clutching at straws.
Not ready. Neurotic, paranoid, incomplete.
And yet I need someone. It matters not
That my glass slippers will crush your willing feet.
We'll force them on.
Be my intermediate, my bridge, my hungry one,
Until the scales fall from my eyes or Cinders comes along,
Or I adjust to living life alone.

John Tirebuck

Lonely Bachelor Seeks . . .

It started as a basic urge of lust -
To meet a woman, and to have some fun;
Someone I'd use callously - then leave.
'Carpe diem - that's what life's about,'
I said. Then you - you answered my advertisement;
You came into my life - upsetting all
My pre-conceived, self-centred philosophy:
'Love' you said, is not centripetal -
But centrifugal - seeking not itself;
And then - you stole my heart, and walked away . . .

Patrick Macken

Farmer Seeks

Farmer seeks shepherdess with own feather bed
Dogs not objected, two or three if fed.
Photo of farm exchanged for one of you
One of me in last week's paper with prize ewe.
Mam says, I am a loving sort of boy
I would like a woman, same shape as Barbie toy.
My hobby is gathering in my sheep
Romance offered, non-smoking, fast walking, Bo-Peep.
Main factor imperative if to be wife
You must have an income settled on me for life.

Alf Jones

Gentle-Man

If you're rich, if you're poor;
I really don't care at all.
If you're ugly, I won't mind;
Just as long as you are kind.
I won't mention colour or creed;
Hope you've not gone to seed.
Then maybe with lots of laughter,
Together we'll live;
Forever After.

V A Johnson

Footsteps

I heard your fading footsteps,
But the darkness shut me in,
I called, but in a whisper,
For I knew that you had gone.

Your voice I cannot hear now,
Lost words searched for - but in vain,
There is no face, no laughter -
All are now beyond recall.

Yet sometimes when I am dreaming,
And the past can have no hold,
I hear footsteps returning:
My Love is coming home.

Ronald Fiske

Male Graduate

Male graduate, thirty-six,
Funny, friendly, likes the flicks,
Theatre, walking and music's
Charms from Bach to Bix.
Love life is in need of fix
So write please poetess (with pics).

Peter Higginbotham

Lonely Hearts

They wrote to a lonely hearts club
Each as a last resource
Neither with hope it would happen
But magic took its course.
He was a Cornish fisherman
She from the Hebrides,
They'd never have met -
They'd be waiting yet
If they hadn't applied
Bill would not have his bride.

K J Earnshaw

At These Words

At these words please pause awhile
Perchance to see good fortune smile
Though at this time when trust comes hard
With constant need to be on guard
Trusting take this outstretched hand
Of one whose good intent will stand
For the smallest spark can start a fire
Of mutual love that both desire
A true liaison free from strife
That may with hope endure for life.

Derick Atkins

Different Aspects of Love

In life we all have 'ups and downs',
Some dark days causing 'many frowns',
Bright days too - enter our lives,
Bringing romance, and love - husbands and wives.

A steady relationship, with a view to marriage,
Bride and groom - in a horse and carriage,
Or - a friend - suffice - 'sharing fun times' - and then . . .
Returning alone to 'their own little den'.

Whichever the choice - resting entirely with you,
Choose someone who enjoys the same things that you do.

Betty M Bennett

My Kind of Love

Is the love that I want like you read in a book?
That makes you feel good and care how you look,
Where romance blossoms and there's marriage in mind.
Do I really want a love of this kind?
Or do I just need a friend who's good and true?
Someone I can trust and tell troubles to.
Who says I look good and makes me feel so,
Is always full of life and on the go,
I think this is for me so I'll settle for this,
For I'm not ready for marriage and Wedded Bliss.

Margaret Platt

Longing

Arms to enfold me
To hug and to hold me,
Someone to share,
And show that you care,
A shoulder to cry on,
A man to rely on,
A twining of fingers,
A passion that lingers,
Then my love I would give
For as long as I live

Kathy Sherratt

The Waiting Game

I'm older now, and, growing wise,
Thought perhaps I'd advertise.
I saw the ad - it looked quite good;
Imagined ladies in each neighbourhood
Leaving all their chores 'til later,
Gladly putting pen to paper.
There's one I've pictured often now
With soft brown hair and placid brow.
But weeks have passed - I'd best forget her,
For strangely, I've not had one letter.

Lewis des Brisay

Destiny

Penning the letter that
Would change my future,
The clock ticks on.
Perhaps you have decided
You're not for me.
But you are my other
Half; Don't you see.
We fit together
Like lock and key.

Norma Williams

Personal Column

Smart young thing of Seventy-three
Seeks handsome male for company.
He needn't be the virile type
For what I want don't need much hype
Just a wad of notes to take me places
Shopping sprees, days at The Races
I'll cook him things like Mother made
Stews, Spotted Dick, fresh lemonade
Bread and Butter Pudding, Apple Pie
I've enclosed a stamp for quick reply.

Gwyneth Tilley

Entice

I own sixteen acres and a few dozen sheep
On a north facing hillside where Winters are bleak
With a house at the end of a long lonely track
Whose roof is of shingle that slopes at the back
But the quilt is old fashioned and really quite grand
Made and embroidered by my late mother's hand
Creating space that's secure, safe, secret and warm
Two souls could seek shelter from tempest or storm
I'm in need of some comfort, love would be nice
Is there anyone out there this ad would entice.

Mair H Thomas

Putting Out Her Stall

She likes to smoke, enjoys a drink.
Too cultured for the kitchen sink.
Loves eating out and holidays,
Theatre trips and risqué plays.
Prattles small talk, artlessly,
Makes responses, carelessly.
Yet has the most provoking smile,
Attracts attention, all the while.
Life's never dull when she's around
Your feet will never touch the ground.

Stan Taylor

Box No H.O.P.E.

Entertainment is rarely so pure
as delving in classified ads;
how can a lonely heart be 'fun and lively'
'suave-gent' - a masquerading lager lad.

It's a big risk, to trust and believe
these fifteen word lives;
the homely thirty-somethings are probably
advertising alongside their lonely wives.
Yet why are you magnetic, or is it just me:
desperate and pathetic - but not that lonely!

Simone Eade

Searching for Love

I wonder if you will be there today
Nestled within the newspaper lines,
For I am desperately seeking that special person
Who is so very hard to find.
Someone who will run barefoot with me in the summer rain,
Who'll sit with me upon the beach at night
When the moon lights up the sky,
Listening with me to the waves gently lapping at the rocks nearby,
I want someone to share with me all the magical things in life,
I want so much not to be all alone, but to be somebody's wife.

Lesley Franklin

New Man

I'm not looking for a frog,
or a prince, or superman,
I'm looking for a partner
who'll accept me as I am,
a joker who can make me laugh
when I've had a long, hard day,
someone who thinks for himself,
but who'll let me have my say.
If you'd like to be my new man,
please ring me as soon as you can.

Sue Challand

My Lonely Heart

My heart is forlorn
With tears I have cried
Though I search for you
Still you hide.

I know you are out there
The one for me
You're loving and caring
And cute as can be.

Open your eyes, my words will impart
Just how lonely is this lonely heart.

Ann C Thomas

I'm Happy Free and Easy

I'm happy and free and easy
I live in a world of my own
I really have to admit it
My life has never been my own.
I need someone to share me
I hate living a life by myself,
Is there someone out there who is lonely
And needs my warm comfortable self?

D T Beeken

Wanted

I want to meet someone, just ordinary like me,
Who would think I was special
And take me to tea.
I'd like a companion who could understand
How I was thinking, and hold my hand,
And perhaps as we grew closer, and we
Both felt the same
We might even get married and set up a home,
And so through life, we'd go on together
Losing ourselves and finding each other
And I'd be so happy for others to see
That he wasn't just ordinary, but special for me.

Marian Evans

Young at Heart

Every morning without fail
I go and buy the 'Western Mail'.
'Lonely Hearts' is on page three,
Could there be someone for me?
I read the ads and contemplate,
Will I find the perfect mate?
Fat or tall, thin or short,
I'm looking for a real sport.
A toy boy I can call all mine,
Who'll suit a playful eighty-nine.

Maureen Jones

Bohemian Rhapsody

Fat bottomed girl
Ardent fan of Freddie Mercury,
Wants to break free
To spend the remaining days of her life in Barcelona.
Could you set her bicycle pedals awhirl?
Play Flash Gordon to her Dale Arden
In Spanish Catelonia,
In a moonlit fountain garden,
Where coloured water jets, under pressure,
Dance to the rhythms of Pain Is So Close to Pleasure.

Jan Ferrierr

Someone

I'm looking for a sweetheart - who am I searching for
Someone nice and steady just me he will adore
Someone who could be my friend and share my hopes my dreams
Someone very special - who knows what true love means,
Someone who is full of life and likes to have some fun
I feel I have been searching - since time on Earth begun,
As I turn the pages there's someone I could meet
He has all the qualities to make my life complete,
Maybe - we will get married he's all I'm looking for
At last someone to kiss goodnight - I could not ask for more.

Hazel M Foster

The Search

Somewhere out there must be the one,
Who could make my world complete,
On looking through the wanted column,
Was the person I wished to meet,
With music, gardening and walking,
Our interests were the same,
So we arranged a meeting,
I got to know his name,
Now we're in the twilight of our years,
I don't have to search again.

Patricia Short

A Soul Companion

A soul companion is rare and sweet,
A gift, to cherish, which makes your heart, beat.

Sharing and caring, laughing and crying.
Happiness enveloped, in spirits, intwining.

Magical moments, shared with each other
Are, priceless treasures, to savour, forever.

Love, has no measure, if strong and deep,
awaiting with patience, to endlessly keep.
A glorious treasure, sent from above, worn
through life, a gift, to, Behold.

J E Gilbert

Wanted

Wanted, someone who is sincere.
One who could make a heart sing.
Aware that the moment you're born you're somebody.
That life is a wonderful thing.
Grateful for wonders to be seen in this world.
Different foods to be tasted.
Applauding those who entertain readily.
No talent you see need be wasted.
A sense of humour, patient and free.
If you add up to these things, please call me.

Violette Edwards

Box 204

Middle aged professional gent seeks Goddess to adore,
So Helen or Aphrodite, reply to 204

Own home, car and caravan, the country to explore,
So Gypsy Jean or Carmen, reply to 204

For friendship, fun and romance, all it holds in store,
Send a photo and five pounds, reply to 204

If you are free on Friday, and want to know me more,
The wife's away with the kids, reply to 204.

William Patrick Hayles

Answer to a Dream?

I saw an ad: from 'lonely gent'
Could this be my 'heaven sent'
We liked to travel, home, abroad,
This touched in me a matching chord.
And like me he hoped for love,
A caring partner from 'Above'?
He liked a garden, liked to walk,
Liked to chat and have a talk.
(Perhaps we'd share a cosy home
This from which, we'd rarely roam!)

Doris J Baldwin

There Must be

There must be someone, somewhere,
Who longs the same as I
For a friend to care, a friend to share
Their days as time goes by.
Then if our friendship should in time
Turn into something more,
It will really suit me fine.
As that's what I hope for.

P Harris

Where is His Wife?

I put a personal ad in the classified section,
Hoping to find someone to show me affection,
This guy got in touch, my mind was in a whirl,
What did he want from this ordinary girl.

I started to doubt what I had done,
It all started out as a bit of fun,
Too late now, I'm meeting him at two,
I'm a wee bit nervous, well you would be too!

He says he's perfect, intelligent, likes the good things in life,
Well if he's that damn good, where is his wife?

Jacqui Weeks